together

photography inspiring poetry

Photographs by Antoinette LeCouteur

Poems by Peter Dudley

Copyright © 2023 by Peter Dudley and Antoinette LeCouteur
All Rights Reserved

No part of this book may be reproduced or retransmitted in any form or by any means, electronic or mechanical, without written permission of the publisher and the authors.

Requests and inquiries may be sent to admin@graybearcoaching.com. Authors are available for speaking and events.

Cover Art: Peter Dudley and Antoinette LeCouteur

Published by Gray Bear Publications, an imprint of
Gray Bear Coaching, LLC
2120 Contra Costa Blvd #1021, Pleasant Hill, CA 94523
graybearpublications.com

This book is also available as an ebook.

ISBN: 979-8-9876637-0-7

dedication

For all those who seek beauty and joy in the everyday places and moments.

Introduction

This is not a typical book of poetry or photography.

We didn't set out with a vision. In fact, neither of us remembers exactly how this all started. A conversation about where artistic inspiration comes from, perhaps.

What we do remember is that just around New Year's 2022, Antoinette sent Peter a photo she'd taken during a walk they took together in Lafayette, California… and Peter wrote a poem inspired by that photo.

We did it again the next week, and the next. Each week a picture, and each week a poem.

It became a special way for us to connect. We lived an hour apart, and the Omicron variant of COVID-19 was surging. Then, when Antoinette went to Oregon for two months at the end of February to support her family, our weekly artistic practice became a touchpoint of positivity for us through a difficult time.

It also grew into more than that. Together we found that the collaboration created a unique third piece of art, different from just the photograph or poem on its own. And we delighted in discovering how we each saw different things in the same picture, and then how the pairing again changed our outlook on our own part of the creation.

Over the months, the way we approached each week evolved. For Peter, each poem was a challenge not just in pulling out the feelings and imagery the photo inspired in him, but also in looking at each photo in an unexpected way. That's how a bouquet of flowers becomes a mosh pit, or a birdhouse becomes a reflection on aging and loss. Peter also wanted to mix up the styles and make sure he didn't simply write the same poem week in and week out. Sometimes the words flowed freely. Other times, a short poem took hours, or days, to draft.

As the year went on, Antoinette also began setting some rules for herself. Each picture would symbolically capture whatever momentous thing was happening that week—a death in the family, or the birth of a dear friend's first child. She intentionally included a diversity of natural and man-made subjects, and apart from the picture of our hands on the day she returned from two months away, no people appear in any of the pictures.

Although some tweaking of the pictures and minor editing of the poems took place in building this book, we stayed true to the originals. They are, in essence, what we created in the moment.

What's really different about this book is that the photographer did not set out to publish a book of photography, and the poet did not set out to publish a collection of poems.

We simply began playing this game of joint creation together, and sometime around September we began to realize that we were accidentally building something special.

We hope you find it special, too.

We hope you contemplate a picture, then read the poem and see how it changes your view of that picture.

We hope you read a poem and find your own meaning in it, then look at the picture and see how that changes the poem for you.

We hope it inspires you to begin, or to reignite, your own artistic practices, no matter what art form you love. You never know what you might accidentally end up creating.

And, we hope you'll connect with us and share your thoughts. We truly would love to hear from you.

Peter & Antoinette

Forgetting December

Memories of you
melt down these walls
in the smudged strokes
of an over-soaked brush
pressed too hard
against the wood

a childlike urgency
haunts these colors
swaying in the air
with the hollow wind

a vacant reminder
of the time
when color mattered
and the days ran short

Welcome Home
Lafayette, California

Week 1

The Great Resignation

How does the first leaf decide
That autumn has begun?
Just one among billions
It clings to its perch
Clutching at raindrops
Jostling in the breeze
Playing shadows upon the grass
A great canopy of photosynthesis

What makes that first leaf decide
To try on something different
A flicker of gold at the edge
A haughty splash of rouge
Carefree and dapper
Exhilirating and liberating
Pushing the limits of convention
Until all its neighbors
In a riot of color and glee
Leap from the gray branches
And tumble together
To heap in breathless gaity
Grinning up through the barren branches
At the laughing stars above

Golden Carpet
Noe Valley, San Francisco, California

Week 2

Transitions

At the apex of the arcing bridge
You pause
Expecting, I suppose,
Some perspective,
Having come,
As you have,
Halfway across the chasm

Not quite leaving behind
Your slowly blurring past
Not quite able to see
The pixellated future

In this moment
Of dizzying *middleness*
The only things that seem clear
Are the cold steel of the dust-painted railing
Wrapped tight in your fingers
And the long shadows of an afternoon in decline
And the seductive pull
Of a sideways
Escape

Path Ahead
Fallen Bridge Park, San Francisco, California

Week 3

Different

A field of sameness
Stretching over the hill
A field so uniformly green
It's as if it had been painted
In one color by a single brush
With only a ghostly suggestion
Of shadows in the brush strokes

You rise
Unique
An island - isolated
A firework - brilliant
An anomaly - different

All attention snaps your way
Passers-by take photographs
With shallow depth of field
Blending everything else
Everyone else
Into a background blur
Until the world around you
Melts away
Like dreams
At sunrise.

First of the Year
Howe Homestead Park, Walnut Creek, California

Week 4

Island Barstools

When the tourists have gone home
To their grayscapes of winter
Where twilight begins at sunrise
And night descends early
Where words of love struggle through earmuffs
And mittens turn caresses into woolen bludgeons
Where ice is for windshields, not daiquiris
And a flushed face means someone
Has been shoveling snow

Do you think they see us in their thoughts
In the ruby and emerald glow of a traffic light
In the flashing amber of snowplow signals
In the frantic tango of a couple slipping on black ice

Do you think they turn up the furnace
Pull down the blinds
Slip into a bikini
Close their eyes
And think
Of us?

Take a Seat
Healdsburg, California

Week 5

One Hundred Years

When I was little, maybe three
I dug a hole to plant a tree.
The field was empty as coud be.
The older kids all laughed at me.

As I went out, I heard them shout
"It's just an acorn! Throw it out!
You're wasting time! It cannot sprout!
There will be fire! Also drought!"

But in a year, that little tree
Was nearly just as tall as me.
And I watched on in silent glee
As it grew slow but steadily.

I left for school, and then for war
A marriage, children, grandkids—four!
While back at home, that tree grew more
And dropped its acorns to the floor.

And now I am a hundred-three.
I'm heading home at last to see
If it's still there, that little tree
And if it still remembers me.

Grateful for Nature
Hendy Woods State Park, California

Week 6

Counting Shadows

What was it
That carried you here
To this desolate place
Where grains of desert sand skip
From dune-top to dune-top
And ricochet off your face
To mark you with a billion
Microscopic sunburns

They come
On a scorching wind
As rhythmic as ocean waves
Curling up from memory
Stretching toward consciousness
Only to thin and flatten
And melt again
Into the insatiable sand

What was it
In the cold wet of before
The waiting, the wishing
The slow pendulum
Rhythmic
As someone else's heartbeat
Predictable as the moon
Rocking as a mother rocks a baby
Pulling reality away
One fingernail at a time

It all seems so far away now
So unbearably far
And you may still have far to go
If only you could remember
Where you came from
And what brought you here

Sand and Sea
Fort Funston, near San Francisco, California

Week 7

Excelsior

A window-washer fell
from that building

that building, just there

he fell to the sidewalk
near the corner
where the shawarma truck
I've always meant to try
parks at lunchtime

but it wasn't lunchtime

eight stories
can you imagine

how much time did he have
to think about life
to think about death
to think about all the things
he might never get to do

I heard he survived
broke both his legs
but that's just a rumor

every morning
we walk our monotone commute
looking straight ahead
not at that building
not at that sidewalk
not even at each other
all of us a slow motion blur
gray phantoms melting invisibly
against a grayer background

and then one day this guy
this one guy
in banana-yellow pants
glows into existence
from somewhere ahead
and we avoid him
as if yellow might be contagious

but a part of me notices
I remember the window washer
with his broken legs
and I wonder what color pants
he wears now
and I think

today

I will have shawarma for lunch

Rise Anew
Eugene, Oregon

Week 8

Teardrop

in the spring
of a new century
the world dangles
upside-down
stretched
swollen
clinging to a past
it does not understand

we wait
breathless
for the fall
into nonexistence
or transformation

and it feels like
maybe
we've been here before

Seeing Through the Rain
Eugene, Oregon

Week 9

Pre-Dawn

The steam
Of my beige coffee
In a white mug
On a brown table
Presses up the window
With a caress of fog
And impermanence
Like a spectral cat
Gazing with expectation
Through the glass
At a silvered world

The frosted grass will endure
And the coffee will cool
And I will stare
Across the blank table
At your chair
Empty
Waiting for the sunrise

Just like yesterday.

Frost Melts
Eugene, Oregon

Week 10

Fly Again

After the lightning has faded
When the thunder is a dull memory
Rest awhile in my arms
Allow me to be
Your faded fleece blanket warm from the dryer
Your chipped teacup blooming lavender
A forgotten soft melody resurfacing

Until the sun pushes through the clouds
And the teardrops begin to dry up
And you feel the strength to crack open your shell
To test your battered wings once more
Against the cruel and unpredictable wind

Lucky Lady
Eugene, Oregon

Week 11

Love At First Sight

She burst through the crepe paper wall
In the manner of a cat making a rapid escape
From a fall into the toilet

Scattering torn paper
And terrified busboys
With one strappy sandal
Swinging in violent arcs
From her long, gray hair
And another gripped tight
Between bared teeth

And I wondered for a moment
If the crimson streak
Across her white camisole
Was blood
Until with fire in her eyes
She slid to a stockinged stop
And held up a glass
And announced
To the stunned diners
That the sandals
Belonged to someone named Kate
And the red wine
Currently soaking into her skin
Was not hers
For she was drinking white
And had not spilled a drop.

Sunshine on My Face
Eugene, Oregon

Week 12

Nothing Lasts Forever

I knew you didn't believe the words
When you recited them once more
In a monotone as gray as pavement
As if the repetition alone
Would convince you of their truth

People say things like that
In times like these

But as you held my hand
In the hospital parking lot
We looked at the ground
Your green Keds already fading
Under the silent clouds
Where footsteps get lost
In the eternal swirling winds

Safe Landing
Walnut Creek, California

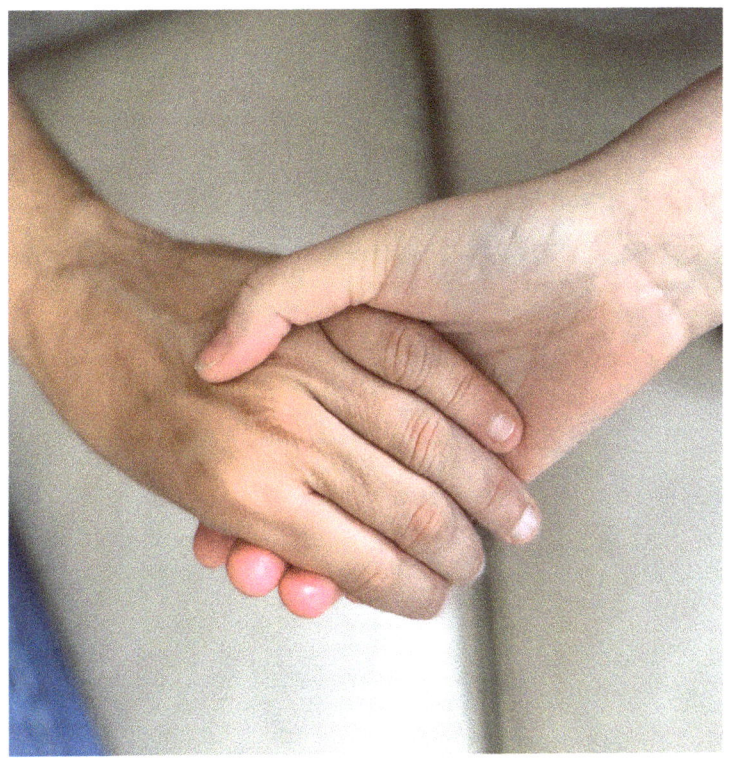

Week 13

Pink Lemonade

These aren't for kids, she purred
In an effervescent half-growl
And I couldn't stop myself
From moistening my lips
With one slow curl of the tongue
As her slender fingers caressed away
The glistening suggestion of sweat
Beginning to rise on her bare neck
Then with one tangy glance
And a calculated quiver of eyelashes
She bent over
And plunged one hand
Into her chest
Causing such a sloshing about
That the ice and water
Slopped over the edge
Soaking the grass
Then she looked up at me
With a tart grin
And a held out one hand
Slowly uncurling her fingers
To expose her shivering rosy palm
And a pale pink ice pop
Lucky you, she said
Pink lemonade
My favorite

Layers Unfolding
Mission District, San Francisco, California

Week 14

Breakup

As the band took the stage
And battered the cramped room
With a hard, pounding beat
We ran out of words
The night's conversation condensing
On the curves of your glass
Where the sultry humidity
Of the nearby dance floor
Pulsating with the fresh sweat of youth
Slammed into the raw truth
Of an icy gin and tonic

With shivers and blurs
The gathering droplets glittered
In refracted reds and blues
As one ice cube settled
With a silent crack
Lost under the forgettable noise
The tips of your numbing fingers
Smeared the sediment of decades
Across the acrylic tabletop

Live Music
Walnut Creek, California

Week 15

A Second Kiss

It was under a deep blue sky
That you had your first kiss
And I made a secret wish
Behind the bank building
Where the teller lady who made change
For the soda machines
Would smoke her Marlboros
And scratch her lottery tickets
During her short afternoon breaks

And ever since that afternoon
Under the deep blue sky
With the peonies blooming
Along the edge of the parking lot
And the tight smells of grilling peppers
Creeping through the alleyway
And your backpack
Pulling your shoulders back
Heavy with your school books
I have thought of that place
As the spot where people make secret wishes
They know will never come true

Time to Celebrate
Walnut Creek, California

Week 16

Glass Tulips

Did the rock know millions of years ago
When it first came to understand it had been created
That after eons of stoic fortitude
Grimly observing seas rising and dying
Noting the comings and sometimes the goings
Of protozoa, of cealocanth,
Of stegosaurus, spider, and squirrel,
Of blue jay and blue spruce
After all that time exposed
Wind-battered and sun-cracked
Each year grinding away the edges just a little more
One day all its pieces and parts
Disintegrated into glistening grit
Would be gathered
Poured and mixed, heated with care
Until all those biting, bitter grains
Would finally let go their hard memories
And melt
To be mixed with color, spread thin
Molded, cut, polished
Into shapes it had once noticed on a nearby hillside
To be gently placed on a windowsill
To relax under the sun's warm afternoon rays

It probably did not know
But perhaps
In secret
It hoped

Tulips for Ellen
San Francisco, California

Week 17

The Crossing Guard

The watcher sits high on its metal cross
Head bobbing, eyes shifting left and right
Gaze flicking from pilgrim to pilgrim
As if tracking a frantic grasshopper
Which leaps from shoulder to shoulder
Seeking the smallest feeling of safety

The watcher scrutinizes with a prejuduce
Born from eons of communal memory
A memory grown from a seed that began rotten
And which embraced rottenness with each season
Sown and re-sown generation after generation
Until rottenness and reality, now indistinguishable,
Became the people's only sustenance

There was a time not yet lost from memory
When the watcher's judgment skipped past me
With only a momentary hesitation
A dark suggestion in the fog of the watcher's mind
A suspicion not yet fully formed
And I was allowed to pass

That was before this year's harvest.

Crossing Guard
Iron Horse Trail, Walnut Creek, California

Week 18

Siblings

"You waddle here, you waddle there,"
Honked Sister Goose in angry tones.
"As if you haven't any care.
You make me weary in my bones!
You'll twist your ankle in those stones!"

But Brother gave a placid stare
And paid no heed to Sister's groans
For he'd been careful to prepare
And could not hear her angry moans
'Cuz he was wearing her headphones.

Flow of Color
Walnut Creek, California

Week 19

Mosh Pit

We flow slowly into the darkness
Jostling and bumping
Like blossoms floating on a stream
Shoulders brushing strange shoulders
Hips grazing strange hips
All the edges tingling
Soaked in the vibrating haze
Pressing together
Tighter and tighter
Until that frozen moment
When all breath stops
Then the explosion
Noise and light and motion
And for a while we become
A singularity of life
A bouquet of humanity
In every color and shape and size
Every hope and anxiety and frailty
Existing together
Beyond the reach of prejudice.

Nature is Beautiful
San Francisco, California

Week 20

On the Wind

September tangles gray
In absent distraction
As we clutch at rainbow memories
And knit our fidgety fingers
To sculpt discordant thoughts
Into a brittle labyrinth
Hoping to delay the numbness
And recall the reluctant brilliance
Which already seeps out
Under the inevitability
Of a winter twilight.

Day Off
Richmond, California

Week 21

Train

The other passengers
Collapse into faded books
Folding their secret minds
Tight between the pages
Their brittle buried faces
Smothered in yellow light
Their twitchy fingers
Confused by the gray rumble
But I look sideways
To feel the cold breath of night
Slip down the window
Slide across my wrists
Writhe around my fingers
Which grip the armrest
With the ferocity of grief
And the futility of memory
And I am keenly aware
Of all the empty spaces
Now occupying my life
As I watch the black hills
Slither into the past

Perfect for Me
San Francisco, California

Week 22

In Search of Between

Is it a nobler thing
To avoid the fiery arrows of judgment
To keep one's head below the ramparts
Settle into a gentle routine of labor and rest
Pretend that peace and familiarity will be enough

Or to strip naked and paint your skin
Raise your flaming torch and set your flag ablaze
Snap the snares tight across the drum
Stampede through the gates
Amid the howl of trumpets and electric guitars
And glare into the roiling, foaming rage
Of a deranged world hurtling to its doom

Colored Over and Made Anew
Santa Cruz, California

Week 23

faithless

blood rises to the top
effervescent
reflecting and refracting
through the fracturing ice
contriving a monochrome rainbow
of crimson, magenta, rose
oozing upward
driven by a feverish delusion

and when false words of forgiveness
have been cast to the floor
and skitter away into dark places
like cockroaches fleeing the light
you will drift discarded and disowned
with only your malformed righteousness
your simmering misunderstood guilt
and the silent knowledge that
when all this has ended
and you face death's bleak eternity
then, in the final reckoning,
you will see that
blood rises to the top

Seeing the True Colors
San Francisco, California

Week 24

On This Push-Pop Afternoon

A threadbare curtain billows
in unsteady lurches
from a half open window
three stories above
its fraying edge snagged on jagged
bent metal of a wheezing
air conditioner
bought off the internet
by the lady who wears a headscarf
to hide her wispy magenta hair.
These sweltering, stagnant days
bring back memories of the shore
watching your mom
in her flip-flops and wide sun hat
pullling lobsters from the pot
oozing steam like dragons
dappled in sunburn red and butter white
while you and I savored the last sticky drops
of push-pops melting onto our fingers
as the tinny jingle of the ice cream truck
faded away with the setting sun.

Boston Art Walk
Boston, Massachussetts

Week 25

Blackout

After the lights went out,
I handed you a matchbook
And the only candle I found
In the drawer by the telephone,
A cranberry-vanilla votive
Partly melted into an old jam jar.
When you yanked
One paper match
From the faded book,
You grimaced.
Just a little, but I noticed,
Even in the dim, red glow
Of the bedside alarm clock,
The only thing illuminating
This rapidly constricting room.
Was it merely the strain
Of the pulling,
Or did your face contort
With the blow
Of a sudden memory,
A punch to that tender spot
In your ego
That you had disguised
So long ago
With makeup and smiles

But secretly kept unhealed By
burying your pain in a drawer
Among thumbtacks and paper clips
And dead batteries
And unused bookmarks
And cranberry-vanilla candles

I may have whispered
"It's time to let it go"
And the sudden flame spitting
From the match
May have glinted in a tear
And I may have felt some hope
In this blackout

But as the candle sputtered
And fake vanilla syruped the room
I watched you pretend
Not to recognize
The name of the Italian restaurant
Rising from the matchbook

And you watched me
Pretend not to see
You slip it back into the drawer
In the table at your bedside.

Love Is Light
Concord, Massachusetts

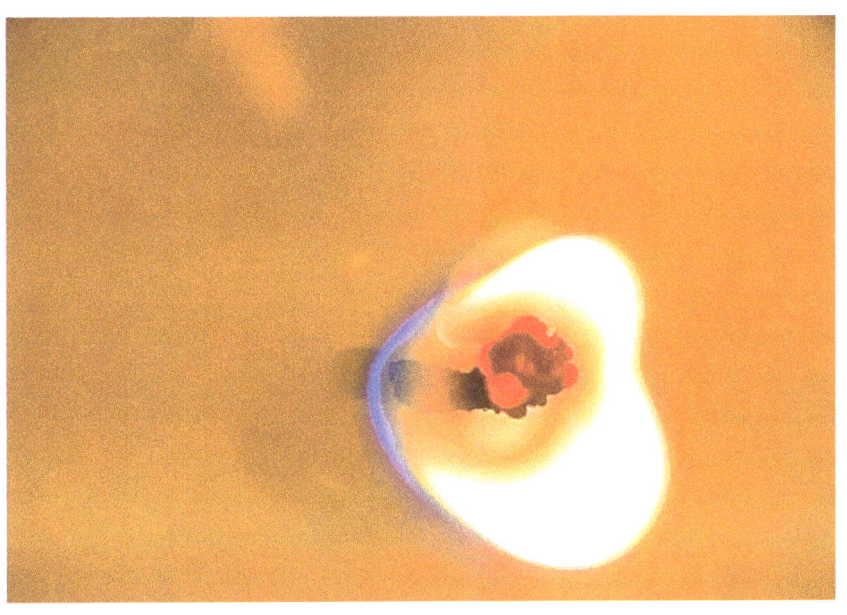

Week 26

Barstools

The leather has darkened
From cocktail cherry red—
Red like the fancy dark cherries
Bartender Mike used to hide
Behind the campari for us,
The cherries with the fancy name
You asked me to pronounce
And then laughed when I said
Luxor or Tuxedo or Toxin—
I never learned the real name
Because you had the best laugh
Light and sparkly and popping
Like prosecco
Pop rocks sprinkled on vodka

Mike keeps telling me
"she'll come back"

But the leather has darkened
Now it's more of an old cabernet
Smooth and sturdy
Fraying in the seams
Weary and brooding and lonely
Or maybe I'm describing myself

I guess that's what happens
With the years
And the absence of laughter
And the steady, reliable
Application of regret

Ice clinks in the empty glass
Cold against my lips
I raise a silent finger for another

Mike winks
He raps a knuckle on the bar

He knows it's the anniversary

"This one's on me" he says

I nod gratitude
He sets two glasses on the bar
Reaches behind the campari
And for the first time in an eternity
He pulls out the fancy cherries

A body slides softly in beside me
And a voice I thought I'd forgotten
Says gently, "Luxardo"

And I feel pop rocks
Being sprinkled on my heart

Home
Hebron, Connecticut

Week 27

Messenger

I walk atop the empty spaces
The in-betweens
Where the currents of the void
Stir death into life
And life into death
Until they blend like white light
A rainbow paradox
Bearing every fragrance ever imagined
And I gather the unending stories
Whispered by the blossoms
To carry them one to the next
And scatter their joys and sorrows
Among the forgotten souls
Wandering in abandoned wastelands
In search of a future they might understand

Summertime
Walnut Creek, California

Week 28

The Dizziness of Staying Still

We lay on the warm September hillside
On tired grass textured brittle and brown
Watching vultures drift across the orange sky

Clouds bleached furrows in the heavens
Leaving behind blurred afterthoughts
Of a stubborn summer wavering on the brink

The clouds, the summer, the grass, and I
Contemplated our mistakes
Meditating on the nature of forgiveness

Days melted into seasons
Seasons stretched into years
Years wheeled into centuries

Until, pinging and clattering one by one
Like ball bearings dropped into a steel bowl
Her words startled me back into existence

Don't fall in, she said.

Don't fall out, I replied.

Swirling in Words
San Francisco, California

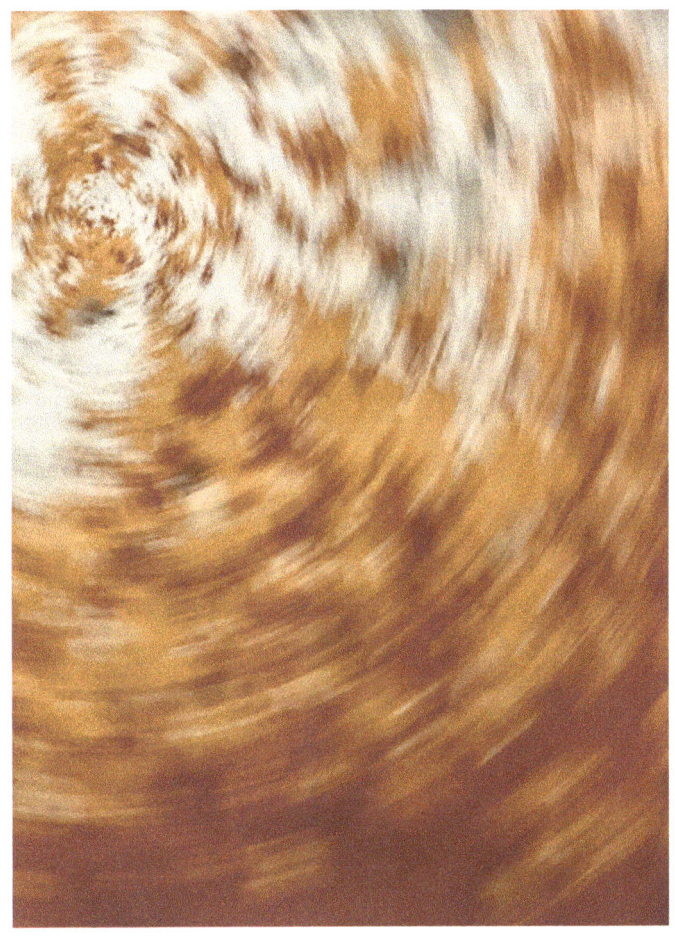

Week 29

Only Now

Only now
In the late afternoon
When the commotion has settled
And the leftovers wait in their boxes
   tucked deep in the back of the fridge
And the cousins have finished renewing promises
   to see each other more often
And all the little grandchildren
With their innumerable siblings
Are already slumped asleep in back seats
As their parents sigh about traffic on the interstate
And wonder again about the gnawing emptiness
They've never quite been able to name
That fills the darkening silence of the car

It's late afternoon
The sun settles itself on the ledge of the horizon
The magnolia outside the window glosses in silhouette
Fresh cut hyacinth infuses the room with tranquility
And the shadows
Like cats
Stretch out their long arms
Reaching for one more moment in the sun
Before welcoming the inevitable peace
Of day's end

Uncertainty
San Francisco, California

Week 30

Opaque

Life's not just a piece of cake
And some days we all need a break
So when my heart begins to ache
I go outside, my break to take

But please don't think that I'm a flake
And if you do a double-take
Just give your head a little shake
And walk on by, for goodness sake

Beautiful Design
Walnut Creek, California

Week 31

She was

She was hopeful.
She was in love.
She was afraid.
She was so many things before

Before the heavens growled with thunder
Before the winds spat their sudden rage
Before the lightning cackled betrayal
And the clouds blackened the sky like bruises

She fled, ashamed.
She wandered, unaware.
She endured the pricking of thickets.
She eluded the stalking of predators.
She survived the advice of the well-intentioned.

After all the peaks and valleys
After all the fictions and lies
After all the bandages and torn scabs
She found that beneath the scars

She still had fear.
She still had love.
She still had hope.
She had so many things
But now she knew a truth
That she had not understood before:

She *was*.

Words Tell a Story All Their Own
Walnut Creek, California

Week 32

orbs

rewind the tape
roll back time
replace what was
with the presence
of nothingness

as the orbs
sweep blackness
through space
the difference between
dark matter and light
becomes immaterial

meaning and purpose
retreat to the shadows
and existence
hangs by threads
from the sepia reality
of this moment

Possibilities
San Francisco, California

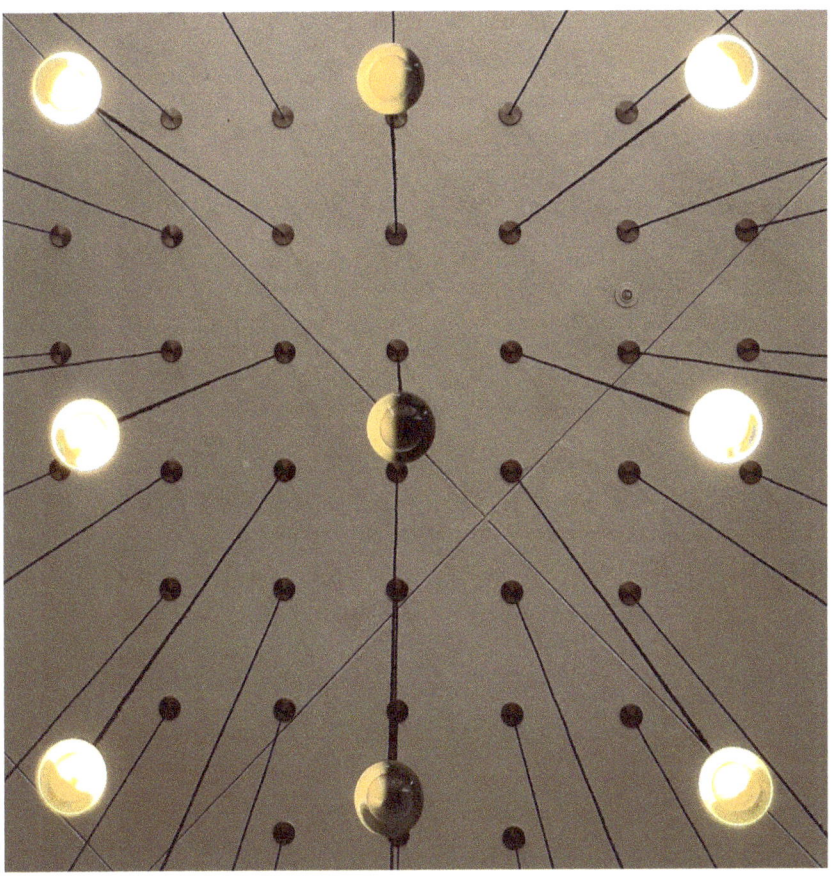

Week 33

Trespassing One Afternoon in The Abandoned Vineyard

Do you remember the taste of the grapes?
Each bite released a tang of history and dust,
Resurrecting the ghosts of forgotten generations
Children giggling through the vines
Ignoring calls from their distant mothers
As they rolled grapes off by the bunch, by the dozen
To cascade over and around their tiny fists
Carelessly unconcerned with the ones lost in the dirt
The air electric with the threat of wasps and summer rain
As they raced back to the big house
And the promise of lemonade and shave ice

Do you remember the taste of the stagnant air
When we wrenched splintered boards from the window casing
Rusted nails protesting in groans, their complaints gritted
With the old-country accents of great-grandfathers
We clambered through into the suggestion of yesterday's youth
Fleeing the ripening storm with its plump, dark clouds
Tumbling to roll among the cobwebs
Like discarded grapes skittering into the shadows
Until you whipped the age-heavy sheet off the ghostly sofa
And we fell together onto its creaky cushions

Sun Kissed
Walnut Creek, California

Week 34

Glide

When the wind is high
Strive for the skies
Press ever upward
Pull toward possibility
Push away the mundane
With all the determination
Your heart can summon

But on a windless day
Tuck your wings
Embrace yourself
Let the water soothe
Absorb the stillness
And glide

Sailing Forward
Avila Beach, California

Week 35

Perspective

I wish I could be there
ten hundred billion years from now
when, having wandered the vast emptiness for eons
these dusts may gather again in some distant place
carrying the patinaed memories of this perfect morning

the aroma of fresh toast crisping the air
children below reuniting with yesterday's friends
their joyful shouts rising from the schoolyard
to drift through the ivoried lace curtain
cushions grown comfortable in their lumpiness
leaning against the creaky wood of the old bench
with its wrinkled and furrowed gingham seat

the sun slipping between us
to glitter playfully in the steam
which pirouettes above
our familiar porcelain mugs

Home Alone
San Francisco, California

Week 36

The Dark Truth of Free Refills

It's an art form I've perfected
Letting his cup get just empty enough
Never fully drained
The last few unsatisfying sips
Not quite gritty enough to shun
Not quite cold enough to discard
Not quite bitter enough to despise

I wait for that singular moment
When his distaste for the dregs
Makes him long for what he had before
He sees the empty space in the cup
And instead of drinking away the remnants
He wishes for the emptiness to be filled again

That's when I arrive
Steaming, percolating

But over time
With each new pour
The sediment accumulates
The porcelain stains
The bitterness thickens
And I fear that one day
When he contemplates the emptiness
He'll decide it's not more of the same he wants
But a whole different cup.

My Morning View
San Francisco, California

Week 37

The Brittle End of Summer

It has that feeling
Like reading a good book
On the train ride home,
A particularly gripping thriller
With a cliffhanger on every page
When you come to a chapter's end
And you look up
Still seeing the story's scene
Still hearing the characters' voices
And slowly
The pounding of your heart
Becomes the clacking of the wheels
And you think how unusually brown the distant hills are
As you watch unfamiliar buildings blur past
And the unrecognized landscape
Glides purple against a silvered horizon
And for a moment you think you're on the wrong train
Or perhaps you've missed your stop
But you aren't, and you haven't
And although you enjoyed the book
As the train sighs slowly into the final station
You suddenly find yourself realizing
You wish you had done more
To enjoy every moment
Of this too short ride.

Seeing Us Through
Walnut Creek, California

Week 38

Passing Grace

Turn toward the brightness, little one
Open your perfect eyes
Slowly, slowly
Spread your yearning arms
Wider, wider
Stand solid and proud
Let your naked feet sink into
The maternal earth
Let her rich loam rise and seep
Between your ticklish toes
Greet the sun's invisible tendrils
Reaching down to entwine your fingers
Warmly, warmly
Welcome the tingling that ripples
From fingertips to soles and back again
The silent harmonies
The infinity of stars
Inviting you to join them
In their limitless enduring grace.

Peaceful Rest Kathy
Eugene, Oregon

Week 39

Insult

She turned without warning
Her taffeta swagger
Swishing on spindly legs
Trembling with rage
Her unsteady retreat
Echoing sharp paces
From daggered heels
Splashing the emptiness
Of her sudden absence
Across the marbled faces
Of an astonished crowd
Left only to wonder
At so much left unsaid
And even more left unheard

Her Favorite Way to Fly
Eugene, Oregon

Week 40

Apple-Stealing Season

You called down to me
"It tastes like a sunset
But without the mint"
Your voice was thick with juice
As the apple's crunch washed into
The crumpling confusion of leaves
I imagined your feet swinging among the branches
And one arm wrapped around the tapered trunk
As I sat below among the damp-darkened moss
Where the snails would wander at night
And all those firework leaves would land
At the end of apple-stealing season
I let my eyes do the almost-close
Blurring the delicious red of the sky
Into a dark blend of syrupy brown
The crisp breeze raised goosebumps
Sliding up under my summer sleeves
As you crunched another bite
And all I could taste was the absence of mint

Change of Seasons
Eugene, Oregon

Week 41

Participate

Lurk in the shadows
If you must
Observe the brilliance of others
From what seems a safe distance
Stifle adventurous words
That clatter and rattle
Clamoring to escape
From your caged imagination
Restrain restless feet
Tapping and twitching
Thrashing toward freedom
From your restrictive bindings
Drain away the colors
Make all shapes uniform
Stop every motion
Descend into stillness
A singularity
Nonexistence

Lurk in the shadows
If you must
But do not linger there long
For in the shadows
You will lose yourself
And deny the world
The joy of knowing
The uniqueness of you.

Colors of Light
Point Richmond, California

Week 42

First Driver's License Photo

It's here at last
I've paid my fee
The car is gassed
I feel so free
I've passed the test
Can't wait to drive
I look my best
Feel so alive
"A picture please"
Sure, happy to!
"And now say cheese"
"Ch… ch… ACHOO!"

Good Clean Fun in Vegas
Las Vegas, Nevada

Week 43

Not Yet

The crows have plucked the sunflowers bare
And the squirrels have buried their nuts
Morning frost silvers the huddled grass
And the brown hills thirst for winter rains
Parents have put away their children's costumes
And car doors and greetings punctuate the nights
Generations congregate in gratitude
I imagine the aromas of baking pie and fresh bread
The calendar turns and the days grow short
And if I engage every brittle sinew of this failing body
I can rise just enough
To grab a brief glimpse of festive lights
Hung too early on other people's houses
Their blurring glow inspires stubbornness
And I reject the inevitable change in season
Balling my fists against the chill
I glower into the winter wind
And declare
Not yet

Falling
Walnut Creek, California

Week 44

Untethered

No haters ever gonna bring me down
I'm surfing the sky
Riding abandon and ozone
I can't hear you, haters
I got clouds in my ears
I can't see you, haters
Sunbursts sparkle my eyes
I'm dancing on airwaves
Ultraviolet undulations
Groovy vibrations
No time for doubt
No patience for flack
Walls are illusions
Can't hold me in
Can't hold me back
Got the whole universe
Right here inside me
So grab your shades
Step up and step in
You can look down any time
But why would you?

Riding the Waves
Austin, Texas

Week 45

Other People's Shoes

At the curving apex of the bridge
That crosses the river at Daniver Street
I paused in mid-commute
Entranced by the uneven ripples
Texturing the water and the sky
Nature and physics dancing
Twirling and swishing away
Leaving gossamer trails that will dissolve into the past
Like the scratches of my footprints
From a thousand evening commutes
Wiped away by thousands of other people's shoes
And the twinkling twilight trees
Electrified with manufactured holiday joy
Glittering along the river's edge
Reminded me of nightclubs long ago
When we twirled and swished together
Without caring where we started
Without knowing where we might end up
Floating on each other's breath
Into song after song after song
And as I stood on the bridge remembering
I glanced up at your window
Third from the far end on the fourth floor
And wondered for the thousandth time
Whose shoes lay beside yours these days
Tucked discretely under your bed
Wiping away the last fading scratches of mine
As I feel myself dissolve into the past

Light the Way
San Antonio, Texas

Week 46

Balcony

Voices mingle and hum
An indistinct fizz of words
Bubbles falling into the sky
Swirling and whirling
Like a rain of prism starlings
Bending and refracting thought
Stretching what had been known
Into inside-out uncertainty
Until the whole world blurs and flips
At the sharp edge of refraction
To split truth from reality
And scatter the unfamiliar fragments
Across a newly honest landscape

Gratitude
San Francisco, California

Week 47

Tideline

A lightning moment exists
When the fiery flow you've been riding
Collides with the cold ebb of reality
In an undeniable popping of flashbulbs

That heady, liquid rush of life
Glittering with the rhythm of waves
Driving beats and slashing crescendos
Flaming ruins in your wake
Acrid with the exhilaration of escape
Gets turned over and under and over again
Tumbling curling crashing
Freezing time and all thought
Until your rebellious heartbeat slows
To echo the swirl of the galaxy
And you find yourself drifting
In the comfortable disorientation
Of what feels like nonexistence
But which you will come to find
Has been the purpose you've been seeking
Since before the stars were conceived

Welcome to the World, Little One
Walnut Creek, California

Week 48

Blank Slate

I will point myself at the unknown
And stride into the unmapped spaces
Breathe in the undiscovered ideas
Feel their acid heat in my guts
Let the chlorine splash of newness
Wash away grime and grease
I will spit out the putrid breath held in so long
And uncloud my eyes from the mists of my past
Break free from the clutch of graveyard decay
And push my charge on into the light
Until the judgmental moans of ancestors
Blanch on the bare stone like distant echoes
And the condemnation of all my past selves
Vanishes under the brilliance of pure possibility.

Left an Impression
Walnut Creek, California

Week 49

Strung Out

Inspired toward greatness
I looked for my reflection
In the gleaming golden guise
Of the successful man
I stood dazzled and open-mouthed
Distracted by his shine and polish
The long line of his achievements
The perfect pitch of his voice
The flawless form of his brand
And I saw possibility
I saw myself

But

The longer I gazed
The more distorted my reflection became
The more the mask cracked
Until the glitter chipped away
And the facade shattered into shards
To reveal a hollow void
And a fraying string of empty hurrahs
Being dragged behind him
Through the thinning mud

So I turned away

For this was not
The kind of greatness
To which I aspired

Beauty Found
Walnut Creek, California

Week 50

Wishing for June

A lively pair of violins harmonize
In arcs and curves and swooping leaps
Their animated passion
Tracing musical rainbows
Riffling through tall grasses
In the keen sunshine
The day overflowing with summer
Perfumed with lilac and coffee
Lying on a coarse blanket
With the gentle pulse
Of your untroubled heartbeat
Soaking through my skin

It all seems so far away
On this drear day in winter
As I peck away at spreadsheets
And raindrops rap-tap my window
And outside a garbage truck groans
Then hurls its dumpster to the curb
In one massive metallic clang
Which reverberates up and down
The vacant, rain-gusted city street

Long Day, Long Year
Walnut Creek, California

Week 51

Behind Closed Doors

We called it "condo hell."

That long stretch of apartments between the highway and the creek
The buildings dropped in place like children's wooden blocks
In the most efficient arrangement for the parking of people's cars.

Painted in undercooked pancake brown and wilting watercolor tulip
These boxes deflected words like *beauty* which washed off
Like rainwater through downspouts and French drains.

Occasionally I would spy a hunched resident rushing
From carport to door or the reverse, collar up, eyes down
As if wishing not to be caught outside.

At holidays, wreaths might appear on doors.

I often wondered what I might witness if those doors opened
And the full rich diversity locked so secretly away came erupting out

Exotic spices and foreign accents
Laughter and photographs
Yellowing wedding dresses tucked in boxes under beds
Tears falling after a call from the doctor
Cribs and carseats mid-assembly
Cheers and curses in team colors
Brush strokes on canvas

Complete lives crammed inside blank boxes
Packed and stacked and set aside
While the world hurries past, seemingly intent on not finding out.

A Year Painted with All The Colors
San Francisco, California

Week 52

About The Photographs

Week 1 **Welcome Home**

Lafayette, California
A homemade, wooden birdhouse with a heart shaped door hangs in a tree. It's decorated by a multi-colored splash of paint and highlighted by a beam of sunlight.

Week 2 **Golden Carpet**

Noe Valley, San Francisco, California
A plethora of golden ginkgo leaves spread fallen across a concrete sidewalk. Many are freshly fallen, and some are in varying stages of decay.

Week 3 **Path Ahead**

Fallen Bridge Park, San Francisco, California
The blue railing of a footbridge over a freeway, with the crisscross shadow of a faded turquoise chain link fence falling across it. The footbridge blurs as it descends to the continuing path.

Week 4   **First of the Year**

Howe Homestead Park, Walnut Creek, California
A single sunlit orange California poppy in closeup on a hillside of green grass.

Week 5   **Take a Seat**

Healdsburg, California
Eight primary-colored metal stools in a row outdoors on a brick and concrete patio facing a stone-topped counter. The stools are purple, orange, red, yellow, green, light blue, medium blue, and purple.

Week 6   **Grateful for Nature**

Hendy Woods State Park, California
A view from the ground looking up at the blue sky through a stand of old growth coast redwood trees, with the sun glinting through the branches.

Week 7   **Sand and Sea**

Fort Funston, near San Francisco, California
A lone sand dollar protrudes from the brown sand of the beach, which stretches into a blurring horizon where it is difficult to see where the ocean begins.

Week 8   **Rise Anew**

Eugene, Oregon
A purple crocus with three blossoms rising from the green grass, with the afternoon sunlight lighting up the petals.

Week 9   Seeing Through the Rain

Eugene, Oregon
A raindrop hangs from the bottom of a magenta flowering plum bud in closeup, containing an upside-down image of a lawn and house beyond.

Week 10   Frost Melts

Eugene, Oregon
A stretch of lawn in early morning light, bordered by a wooden fence, with the grass covered in a thick, white frost.

Week 11   Lucky Lady

Eugene, Oregon
A bright red, seven-spot ladybird beetle nestled in the curve of a clover leaf, with glistening dew all around on the surrounding grass and leaves.

Week 12   Sunshine on My Face

Eugene, Oregon
A closeup on a white Magnolia stellata flower in morning sunlight. The pale pink striped petals curl away from the center like crepe paper.

Week 13   Safe Landing

Walnut Creek, California
Two hands, one male and one female, clasped together over the blurred cushions of a white sofa.

Week 14   **Layers Unfolding**
San Francisco, California
A close-up of the peach-colored petals of a rose unfurling in layered folds with the petals' veins visible.

Week 15   **Live Music**
Walnut Creek, California
Two glass tumblers on a reflective table in a dark bar with bokeh color lights in the background. One glass is blurred; the other is in focus, half-filled with a clear ice-cold drink and a lime wedge.

Week 16   **Time to Celebrate**
Walnut Creek, California
Looking up between two buildings–one brick and one white–to see crisscrossing garlands of festive, colorful paper flowers, tassels, and hanging lights, with the clear blue sky beyond.

Week 17   **Tulips for Ellen**
San Francisco, California
A closeup of a bouquet of sunlit, translucent magenta tulip flowers with green leaves. The background is a blurred white curtain across a sunny kitchen window.

Week 18   **Crossing Guard**
Iron Horse Trail, Walnut Creek, California
From below, a lone crow sits atop a crossing of rusting metal beams with a blue sky in the background.

Week 19   Flow of Color

Walnut Creek, California
Two Canada geese wade in the low water of a creek, dappled with a patchwork of yellow, among reflections of the trees and sky. The creek stretches into the distance, with pebbly and rocky banks overgrown with green foliage.

Week 20   Nature Is Beautiful

San Francisco, California
A vivid mixed bouquet of flowers, wrapped in brown paper for sale at a shop. The head of a sunflower dominates the foreground. The bouquet is a rainbow of color with green eucalyptus, magenta hydrangeas, blue larkspurs, yellow lilies, purple Love-in-a-mist, and pink roses.

Week 21   Day Off

Richmond, California
In the background, the water of the San Francisco Bay with Marin County in the distance. In the foreground, one part of a public-art sculpture of a sphere made up of twisting, snaking metal strands. The day is gray and chilly.

Week 22   Perfect for Me

San Francisco, California
A closeup of an abundant display of peony flowers in several shades of pink, some opened and some closed.

Week 23   **Colored Over and Made Anew**

Santa Cruz, California

A flat textured concrete wall painted in vertical stripes of medium blue, red, sky blue, white, yellow, pink, and navy blue.

Week 24   **Seeing the True Colors**

San Francisco, California

A tumbler style water glass up close, with condensation on the outside. Seen through it is a blurred red light which glows lavender colored in the geometric vertical lines of the glass.

Week 25   **Boston Art Walk**

Boston, Massachusetts

A bronze panel in the middle of a brick alleyway. The bronze panel is as long as three bricks, containing a line of lobsters in raised relief blurring from the foreground into the distance.

Week 26   **Love Is Light**

Concord, Massachusetts

A close-up from above of the lit wick of a tea light candle. The center of the wick glows orange-red in the middle of a heart-shaped glow of yellow-white flame.

Week 27 Home

Hebron, Connecticut
A small, temple-like structure stands atop a wooden post in the midst of overgrown greenery with a green lawn behind and a forest blurred in the background. Sitting inside the temple-like house is a small, red cardinal made of wood.

Week 28 Summertime

Walnut Creek, California
A honeybee dusted with yellow pollen walks across the pointy head of a red coneflower. With another flower behind, the image blurs into the greenery in the background.

Week 29 Swirling in Words

San Francisco, California
An abstract swirl of white, orange, and brown, as if colors were put on a spinning surface. The center of the swirl is in the upper left corner of the picture, mostly white, growing darker toward the bottom right.

Week 30 Uncertainty

San Francisco, California
The bottom portion of a wheelchair wheel on a tight-weave beige carpet, with the light behind casting a stretching shadow toward the viewer.

Week 31 Beautiful Design

Walnut Creek, California
A brilliant Gray Hairstreak butterfly with orange markings at the tip of its wings looks poised to take off from the delicate purple verbena blossoms it's perched atop.

Week 32 Words Tell a Story All Their Own

Walnut Creek, California
A closeup of a section of public art. The background is a small section of a topographical map in green and white; across it appears to be a piece of white tape with the words "She was" in a black typewriter font.

Week 33 Possibilities

San Francisco, California
Looking up at a section of beige ceiling, from which are hanging nine white and gold metallic spherical lights on long wires, in a grid like a tic-tac-toe board.

Week 34 Sun Kissed

Walnut Creek, California
In closeup, bunches of plump, full, green and red grapes hang in a vineyard. Warm sunlight highlights those in focus in the background, with those in the foreground blurred.

Week 35 Sailing Forward

Avila Beach, California
A brown pelican floats on a calm stretch of blue water, leaving a small wake behind as it floats from left to right in the picture.

Week 36 **Home Alone**

San Francisco, California
A wooden bench in a kitchen nook with light streaming through a lace curtained window behind it. The bench has a cozy red gingham cushion on the seat, and throw pillows in various patterns and colors cover it.

Week 37 **My Morning View**

San Francisco, California
A handmade coffee mug glows orange in a ray of morning sunshine on the wooden arm of a chair in a backyard garden.

Week 38 **Seeing Us Through**

Walnut Creek, California
Anna's hummingbird with green back, black wings, and white breast sits amid and blends into a chaotic rising of brown and gray-green leaves of a tall grassy plant.

Week 39 **Peaceful Rest Kathy**

Eugene, Oregon
A perfectly shaped, white morning glory blossom with a yellow center and periwinkle highlights faces the camera with its greenery blurred behind it.

Week 40 **Her Favorite Way to Fly**

Eugene, Oregon
In closeup, a bee has just taken flight from a brilliant fuchsia cosmos bloom with a golden center. We see the pollen covered bee from behind just as she is taking flight.

Week 41 Change of Seasons

Eugene, Oregon
A tree is seen from below with hints of blue sky beyond. The leaves of the tree have turned brilliant red and fill the picture with rich color and texture.

Week 42 Colors of Light

Point Richmond, California
Two three-dimensional paper star-shaped lanterns are seen from the side. One is blue and black and white with geometric patterns on it, emerging from the left of the frame to point at the center. The other is blurred in the background and is green and gold and filled with light.

Week 43 Good Clean Fun in Vegas

Las Vegas, Nevada
A lit-up orange jack-o-lantern carved with angry eyes and an open, fanged mouth sits on a white marble table indoors, with blurred white walls behind.

Week 44 Falling

Walnut Creek, California
A single red leaf lies on an empty stretch of pavement dappled with shadows. The leaf is arched in the center, creating a shadow below it.

Week 45   Riding the Waves

Austin, Texas

A rubber duckie with big, red lips and wearing sunglasses floats in a birdbath in front of a white textured wall that is covered with light and shadows in such a way that the wall looks like a cloud-filled sky.

Week 46   Light the Way

San Antonio, Texas

A section of the San Antonio River Walk as seen at dusk from a bridge spanning it. An apartment building rises on the right bank, and trees line the left bank with more buildings in the distance. Several of the trees are covered in white holiday lights. Clouds in the sky glow from the setting sun. The river shows a reflection of the holiday lights and clouds.

Week 47   Gratitude

San Francisco, California

A wine tumbler half filled with rose-colored wine sits atop a wooden railing on a balcony overlooking a broad view of San Francisco. All is blurry except what can be seen through the glass, which is thick in the middle and tapers at the top and bottom. The top portion shows a blue sky with sunlit buildings, and the bottom portion shows the upside-down buildings colored pink by the wine.

Week 48 **Welcome to the World, Little One**

Walnut Creek, California
Millions of tiny white bubbles cover the surface of teal-colored water, forming a crooked line down the middle that looks like a lightning bolt.

Week 49 **Left an Impression**

Walnut Creek, California
A single red maple leaf lies on a patch of gray concrete sidewalk that has been imprinted by dark, leaf-shaped stains where other leaves had lain before.

Week 50 **Beauty Found**

Walnut Creek, California
In close-up, a strand of metallic gold beads lies on the sidewalk. Several of the beads in the foreground have been smashed to tiny shards exposing the string on which the fragile beads are strung. The strand trails around the ground and fades into the background.

Week 51 **Long Day, Long Year**

Walnut Creek, California
A pudgy little bird sits alone on a barren tree branch in silhouette against a pale blue winter sky.

Week 52 **A Year Painted with All the Colors**

San Francisco, California
A bountiful bouquet of flowers and greenery pictured from above fills the frame. A vivid mix of red, pink, orange, yellow, white, purple, and green.

About Peter

Peter is an author and executive coach who tries to make the most of every day. He grew up in Connecticut with summers in Las Vegas, got his electrical engineering degree from UC Berkeley, then went on a long and winding career in startups, nonprofits, and big corporations. Once both his kids were grown, he started Gray Bear Coaching and Gray Bear Publications. Peter has published four novels and a chapter book, and his poetry, short fiction, and professional articles have been published in a wide array of journals and anthologies. Find him at peterdudley.com and graybearcoaching.com.

About Antoinette

Antoinette is a consultant specializing in helping people do good in the world. A theatre major in college and actor early in her career, she transitioned to the world of philanthropy and social impact in the mid-2000s and has helped get hundreds of millions of dollars in employee donations and corporate funds to charities all over the world. In her photography, she captures moments that happen, rarely staging a photograph but preferring to see the world as it is, in unique ways and from new angles. She is especially fond of pollinators, and her camera roll is filled with bees, butterflies, and insects of all types going about their work of maintaining the world. Find her at CreateImpact.world.

www.ingramcontent.com/pod-product-compliance
Lightning Source LLC
LaVergne TN
LVHW061630070526
838199LV00071B/6637